THE TEENAGE WORRIER'S
POCKET GUIDE TO MIND & BODY

T0316118

THE TEENAGE WORRiER'S POCKET GUIDE TO MiND & BODY

Ros Asquith

as Letty Chubb

CORGI

THE TEENAGE WORRIER'S POCKET GUIDE TO MIND & BODY
A CORGI BOOK : 0 552 146439

First publication in Great Britain

PRINTING HISTORY
Corgi edition published 1998

Set in Linotype Garamond by
Phoenix Typesetting Ilkley, West Yorkshire

Corgi Books are published by Transworld Publishers Ltd,
61–63 Uxbridge Road, Ealing, London W5 5SA,
in Australia by Transworld Publishers (Australia) Pty. Ltd,
15–25 Helles Avenue, Moorebank, NSW 2170,
and in New Zealand by Transworld Publishers (NZ) Ltd,
3 William Pickering Drive, Albany, Auckland.

The Random House Group Limited supports The Forest Stewardship
Council® (FSC®), the leading international forest-certification organisation.
Our books carrying the FSC label are printed on FSC®-certified paper.
FSC is the only forest-certification scheme supported by the leading
environmental organisations, including Greenpeace. Our
paper procurement policy can be found at
www.randomhouse.co.uk/environment

Printed and bound in Great Britain by Clays Ltd, St Ives plc

CONTENTS

Bluebird of HAPPINESS

Every silver lining has a CLOUD

Centres of Worry

Brow (OM)

Throat (HAM)

Heart (YAM)
see YOGA at end of buke for explanation

CURDS & WHEY

THE VAST BUKE of CALM Vol XVIIII

Little Flower

Little dog stuff

Little roots

BIRDS don't get depressed

Really?

Letty Chubb, glorying in Nachure and at One with Universe

Feather Bed
Om Sweet Om
Doors-of-Perception
Chakraton
Serendipity-on-Sea
Attitudesville
Nr Futon
Lake of Sagacity
Mount Rapport
Genderfree
IM OK UR OK

Dear Teenage Worrier(s),

Well, hey, wow, chill out, yo dude, respeck. Sitting here on my mountain retreat and gazing down at all you lowly mortals from my dazzling new platitude, I mean altitude, I see how mere specks we are in ye grate Universe; how all our Worries, taken in ye grate context of Eternity, are but tiny morsels to ye Gods of Life. And how, if we can but throw off the sheckles (shouldn't that be shackles? — Ed) of psychic glume, we can fly with the bumblebee and sing with the sparrow.

Now don't go getting the idea that moi, *El Chubb, has entirely changed her character by indulging in some Magickal new technique of meditation, or suddenly discovered I have grate healing Powers, or gone off to Tibet in arms of lissom guru to say 'Zen' — or is it 'Om' — no, but I have, amid the festering glume of LIFE-threatening*

1

WORRY, found a shaft of joy occasionally in dabbling in the hinterland of alternative therapies Etck. It seems to moi that anything, however small, that one can do to stave off the abyss that otherwise threatens the yoof of the planet is worth a try. And, dear reader, when you are Worry-free, you can dispense your calm, your inner joy, your oneness with Yooniverse Etck to other, humbler, needier souls than yrself. Thus the journey I am encouraging you to embark on will be not just a selfish one, but one guaranteed to bring light and peace to help alleviate the sufferings of others (grone, pass sick bag, that's enuf do-gooding – Ed).

Seriously, if you can feel happier yourself, then those around you will also benefit. Wish my own parents wld try some of these remedies to ease the pain of the yuman condition instead of drowning their higher feelings in old-fashioned escapes of booze, fags and V. Bad Temper, though must admit their heart-rending hippified attempts at Meditation, Yoga Etck were not V. Grate success, as I reveal below. Trouble with older generation is they just give up so kwick. I think they suffer from Attention Deficit Disorder.

I believe, if Teenage Worriers cld set V. Good example and practise ancient arts of relaxation Etck, we wld all find our Worries dissolving in sea of Bliss (also, get less cold sores, pustules Etck). However, this humble buke is not a health guide, so don't pore over it hoping to get cures for athlete's foot Etck. It shld be used more as a spirichual awareness type thing.

Yours, dreamily progressing towards Higher Plane. Arg! Where's my hot-water bottle? Lucky rabbit's foot? Teddy? (This may be harder than it looks),

Letty Chubb

Tweet squawk

And now . . . before I plunge headlong into my alphabet of CALM, a few measured werds about the reasons I need this buke (similar, hopefully, to the reasons you too will need it) . . .

Mind Worries

Although I wd like to tell you that writing five thousand bukes about Worry has calmed my seething soul Etck, I must admit to not having quite conquered the vast list of glumes, neuroses, habitz, anxieties, fears, phobias, nervous disorders Etck Etck that continue to plague *moi*.

Frinstance, I still use 'banana' instead of saying or writing the word about dying that rhymes with 'breath'. This makes my skule work V. Difficult, cos obviously I can't just put 'banana' in an essay, so I use all sorts of other methods to avoid using ye dreade word. I wd like to conquer this prob before I do GCSEs, as I often spend hours searching for alternatives which cld result in V. Blank exam papers. Also, sarcastic remarks from teachers about whether phrases like 'Hurtling into the chasm of doom' are suitable for life cycle of tadpole.

I still twist my fringe, stroke my lucky rabbit's foot in times of stress and also have compulsive desire to do small things twice. By small things, I mean, if I drop something, I touch the floor twice, or I turn a light on and off twice Etck. I also Worry about Tragick decline of kindness, future of planet, whether I will get a job, whether I will live to see tomorrow, whether my family will survive Etck Etck, yeech.

So this buke will hopefully be a self-help manual for *moi*, so that by the time I get to the end of it I will have . . . well . . . reached the end of it.

Body Worries

Moi →

Endless. Being lanky Etck. Round folks do not have any sympathy for *moi*, but I looooong to be cuddly. While I know this shows that no-one is ever satisfied and that it it V. Stooopid to whinge on about how you look and there are more important things in life Etck, I still say: just you try looking like a boot-lace with the strength of a flea Etck and see how YOU feel. Also, it is V. Hard for us gurlz who have NO bazooms, waiting for them to come. Also, I measure my nose, tape back my flapping ears, apply zappo to my spotz and zappex to my cold sores daily. Never mind the usual litany of hourly Worries, viz: PMT, brain tumours, nits, athlete's foot, varoukas, ultimately ending in banana Etck Etck. Hopefully, this little tome will enable readers to Worry less about outward appearances and concentrate more on the Inner Self.

5

A Little Note on the Family Worries that occupy my mind and surround my body

* **Father** locked in isolation with computer pretending to write novel but actually playing GOD (computer game where you build own Universe). Scratches measly living by writing Do-It-Yourself articles, which he practises at home to catastrophic effect.

* **Mother** who wants to be artist, but scuffs heels in kiddies section of local library, scorning state of modern edukashun and Worrying about her offspring.

* **Luny brother Benjy** (5), who is phobic about floors, has smile of angel and teeth of *Jaws*.

* **Perfect brother Ashley** (18), at Oxford (whinge, groan, class hatred Etck) learning to be brain surgeon Etck and fighting off swooning females.

* **V Nice granny Chubb**, now retired from cleaning other people's homes, so spends all day hoovering doilies and knitting boleros for *moi*.

* **V. old cat**, who I lurve. Rover (female).

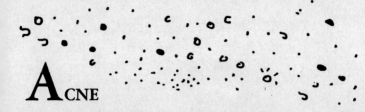

Acne

It is A Well Known Fact that other people not Worrying about the things you Worry about can be V. Worrying. However, there is one thing that all Teenage Worriers agree on Worrying about and this is Acne. (A V. V. tiny minority do not Worry about this because they never get it, but I do not count them as Teenage Worriers at all, or indeed members of The Alleged Yuman Race of any description.)

I believe Acne is prufe that either God does not exist, or that He or She went out for a long lunch when the concept of Teenagers was being worked on, and left it to a bunch of low-grade angels on a *Welfare to Work* scheme. Acne is V. definitely an ailment invented by somebody with a V. sick sense of humour, possibly with extensive experience in terrorist bomb-making factories. Set the time, then guide Innocent Yoof right up to the gates of Adulthood, cackle ye celestial delinquents, rubbing their wings with unholy glee. Let them see Ye Promised Land of Deep Voices, Gropings Behind Bicycle Sheds, Cleavage, Mobile Phones, Driving A Car, Summoning Waiters, Going Bankrupt with Student Loans Etck, and then – *blip! splap! pflurrrp! kerpoww!* – stand back and watch while a meteorite shower of red blobs with pulsating white nuclei

THREE SUCCESSFUL CURES for ACNE

This Teenage Worrier used Chinese herbs...

This Teenage Worrier used TIME...

This Teenage Worrier used L. Chubb's patent ACNE-PACK. Send SAE for bag in four colourways: Beige, sand, pebble or stone. + cheque for £494.99 payable to L. Chubb PLC.

erupts from some dark region of Inner Space within Ye Luckless Teenage Worrier and lays waste to all exposed areas of previously unblemished skin. There are more than 50 types of acne apparently (yeech!), and of course Teenage Worriers suffering from it believe that they have all the variations at the same time.

Akshully, all is not lost. Acne vulgaris is the most common type – so named because a lot of people get it, not because it comes on once you start thinking about SEX. It starts in the sebaceous glands, which are there to put out fatty substances that stop your skin from looking like an old walnut, but which go ballistic when stimulated by all the hormones that start hammering around yr Bod during puberty. Most people get a version with little inflammation, or one with little inflamed pustules that don't leave scars unless you keep hacking at them with yr fingernails, and there are ointments to reduce the inflammation during the year or so (groan) the condition usually lasts. There is a more unpleasant version of acne which attacks the skin deeper down and can leave lasting scars, but V. few Teenage Worriers are unlucky enough to get this – and yr doc may then recommend more drastic measures, inc. ultraviolet light, antibiotics or even hormone treatment. But most cases of acne a) don't look half as bad to others as they do to you, and b) are just another thing you have in common with a large number of yr frendz, and c) go away sooner than you think. Try not to PICK or SQUEEEEEEZE too much though, because a) you might leave permanent marks, and b) yr mum will get fed up with bringing in teams of industrial cleaners to hose down the bathroom mirror.

Acupuncture

V. Ancient technique of Chinese medicine, now V. Popular in right-on muesli circles. It involves having needles stuck in you and works by stimulating energy flows in V. Mysterious pathways in the Bod, identified by mysterious Chinese doctors thousands of years ago  but not the same as the pathways of the Nervous, or Worrying, system. Acupuncture therefore has V. Exciting descriptions of things you might have wrong with you, viz: to whit, *Liver Fire* Etck, which sounds much more interesting than 'tummy upset' or something.

Acupuncture has been proven by suspicious Western scientists Etck to work V. Well on some conditions like certain skin problems, muscle strains

Etck. It doesn't hurt, and fans say it can give you V. Nice feeling of energy, clear head Etck, as well as fixing whatever your prob was. If you fancy it, try it once to see if you like it, but don't believe it can cure all ills or avoid going to a regular doctor for anything that might turn out to be serious.

NB Some people may have an AIDS Worry about infected needles Etck, but if you go to an Acupuncturist who's a member of an accepted practitioners' group you will have no probs because they will sterilize all needles V. Carefully and may even offer to use brand new disposable ones each time.

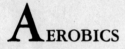AEROBICS

See EXERCISE.

ANALYSTS

Unhappy People are V. good subjects for analysts, as they can find out lots of things that cause unhappiness (ie: Nasty teacher when you were five, nasty parents all the time, no potty training, too much potty training, absence or excess of soya milk Etck Etck) and therefore at least go on being Unhappy with Good Reasons. Happy people sometimes visit analysts too, to iron out some little problem and then realize how many V. V. Big Probs they could be suffering from without realizing it.

For many probs afflicting Teenage Worriers, a

listening ear from a kind and sympathetic person can be the V. best solution. So don't think that seeing a counsellor, analyst, therapist or any other professional means you've failed. Almost everyone needs someone like this at some point in their lives, many of us V. Often. I'm personally saving Deep Analysis for when I'm older and richer, but there is lots of help available to Teenage Worriers who are depressed or Worried. You only have to ask.

See also DEPRESSION.

Apple

According to ye Holy Christian Bible, temptation started here. Since Adam was involved I'm not surprised (phew, cold shower). But it turns out it was only a mouldy old apple. Myself, I was more affected by Snow White than Eve. I still can't eat a shiny red apple, just in case some mirror somewhere is saying 'I'm the Fairest of them All' . . . And some Evil Queen is lurking awaiting her chance to garrotte me. But maybe it wld also mean a Prince is lying in waiting, chance wld be a fine thing.

However, if you wish to be healthy in MIND and BODY, an apple a day will be V. useful (old sayings always best dept).

Ask yrself. Is my LIFE more like this? or this?

Banana

In case you think this buke is turning into fruit salad, this is just little reminder that Banana is the word I am forced, due to phobic terror, to use instead of the one about dying that rhymes with 'breath'. All Teenagers, and especially Teenage Worriers, will spend time Worrying about this subject. The Worries go something like this:

1 What if I die?
2 What if my parents die?
3 What if anyone else I truly love dies?
4 What is banana itself like?

The V. diff thing about this subject is that to be haunted by fear of banana is part of what makes us human. It is the one question to which there are both many answers and no answer. You may have strong religious beliefs, but you cannot know what it is like until you do it.

My own V. Humble contribution is the following V. Comforting thought, which goes like this:

There are two options: a) Either you die and nothing happens, in which case you don't know anything about it, OR: b) You die and something else happens, which is bound to be quite interesting.

The above inclines me to believe that one

shouldn't be fearful, but naturally it doesn't stop anyone Worrying about those they love and imagining how they cld possibly survive without them. Another thing Teenage Worriers do often is to feel responsible for the banana of someone they loved. Examples of this are like when you go out slamming door and saying you hate yr parents and never want to see them again and then that VERY SAME DAY both parents are devoured by white rhino, as in a Roald Dahl book. Or, you have a frend with fatal illness and think if you can sit by her bed every second and do nothing but think of her day and night and never go to loo Etck, she will somehow get better. And she dies while you are having a wee. Sorry to sound glib to any of you who have had experiences similar to these, but Teenage Worriers have a bad habit of blaming themselves. They think: *If I'd phoned her when I said, she wouldn't have taken that bus and then she wouldn't have walked down that street just at the moment that the Jumbo jet fell on her head.* OR: *If I had only got up earlier, I wouldn't have been late to meet him and he wld still be here now instead of under speeding milk-float* Etck.

This kind of Worry can certainly drive you mad, BUT these things are accidents and illnesses. They are NEVER *your* fault. If someone you love has died, *talk* to someone about how you feel. If frendz aren't enuf, try counselling.

← Hope
springs
eternal

15

Bazooms

According to most Teenage Worriers, these are
either too big (chance wld be fine thing, whinge,
glume) or too small. In the case of many Teenage
Worriers, they have not emerged at all. Yet others
are buying vast unwearable cardigans in order to
muzzle and disguise them. In this unwinnable
situation, L. Chubb advises all Teenage Worriers to
take deep breath (espesh in case of those of you with
V. Big ones, har har) and meditate on vastness, not
of yr Bitz, but of universe. Muse also on tininess
(not of your bitz), but of atoms.

Rover's fleas
do not worry
about their
bazooms

We are all titchy blobes whizzing in space, and
whether our even titchier protuberances are big or
small is not — is it? — a thing that shld take up much
of our valuable brain space. This shld, but may not,
stop you Worrying, but I am fed up with sexist
rubbish about bazooms, and, contrary to all my
other bukes on the subject, have promised self to
throw away all those padded bras and learn to enjoy
life without them — and sadly, this means without
any bazooms either, since mine will obv not now
ever come.

A few T-shirts from L. Chubb's Bazoom range.

BERMUDA TRIANGLE

A creeeeeepy area in the Atlantic Ocean off Florida where a number of ships and aircraft have vanished. Also known as the Devil's Triangle, and a source of V. Grate Worry to Teenage Worriers with Travel-Phobia (eg: 'Will I ever HAVE to go to, or through Bermuda?') who have watched too many XYZ FILES Etck. Worriers! Harken to El Chubb: So far, there has been no scientific evidence of any unusual Phenomena involved in the disappearances. So it's not creeeeeepy after all. Yippeeee. Or boo-hoo, depending on mood.

CULTS

Arrgh, glume, POVERTY Etck.

Many unsuspecting idealistic Teenage Worriers have been attracted to cults – organizations that promise an End to War, or starvation or the discovery of a new sisterly love – only to find they are working 25 hours a day for a handful of hot gruel and sleeping on floors while some rich guru is spending their wages on Rolls Royces. If you are seeking spiritual awareness, it's better to go for one of really long-standing well-established religions.

See also RELIGION.

18

Deodorants

There are now so many anti-pong sprays for so many parts of the Body, that I wonder if SEX will soon come to an end, cos no-one will be aroused by erotic smell of opposite gender any more. Limit deodorants to under arms and just wash everything else V. nicely is L. Chubb's advice. Deodorants for naughty Bits can sting and also upset natural balance of fluids Etck.

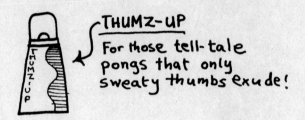

THUMZ-UP

For those tell-tale pongs that only sweaty thumbs exude!

Depression

Granny Gosling says she doesn't believe in Depression. Even when they say on the weather reports that A Severe Depression Is Forming over the Atlantic, she thinks it's a sign that the Elements just ought to pull themselves together. But for just

Wooooo8oooAoo
NOBODY understands
the AGONY of
my SOUL

NB Above is V. NORMAL
result of: PMT, over tiredness,
lack of nice nosh Etck.
Do not Confuse Teenage
Worrier's GLUME with
Depression.

about everybody else, Depression is real enough, and most of us believe we've had at least one, and maybe know somebody who has them so often it's a Major Worry.

But Depression is not just being unhappy because Leonardo di Yum Yum married somebody out of *Babewatch* you could never get to look like even if you ran yr own 24-hours-a-day team of plastic surgeons, or because yr Gerbil doesn't go on its wheel any more, or you think yr Bazooms have akshully got smaller than last month. That is just getting in a Bad Mood and happens to everybody, particularly Teenage Worriers. It's not an illness, because if something nice happens, you can snap out of it, and that can be anything from a bright blue sky, to getting free tickets for Green Spume's 900th farewell concert at *The Hovel*. Even the way you feel if something Really Awful happens to a Frend or someone in yr Family, though it may make you feel Terrible for ages, is not the same as Depression – though it can turn into one, and sometimes you need help to get you over a real shock or bereavement.

A serious Depression goes deeper even than this, and is harder to get rid of. When you are Depressed, you have no energy, and nothing seems worth doing. (According to Only Mother, Teenage Worriers are all like this, but it is not a reliable Medical Judgement.) A Depressed Person may feel V. Slow and Sluggish, be unable to enjoy anything,

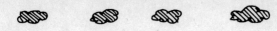

and sometimes unable to sleep (the latter is
definitely a sign that Teenage Worriers As A Hole
don't suffer from it). Or they may alternate between
Slowness and hurtling around bouncing off People
and Thingz like a pinball, which is called Manic-
Depression.

Depression is the most common prob
psychiatrists have to deal with, and it's been known
about since the famous Greek GP, Hippocrates, who
called it melancholia. Stresses of Life can bring it on,
but so can not having enough of certain Vital
Substances that make the brain work, particularly a
chemical called serotonin. Doctors mainly treat
depression with drugs (to restore whatever
Brainstuff yr Bod isn't producing by itself) or
psychotherapy (trying to find out what the real
reason for Yr Misery is) and sometimes both
together. Depression can be eased, and often cured
completely, by the right treatment and it's V. silly
to leave a serious depressive illness untreated.

Diets ← Boo

V. Large numbers of Teenage Worriers are worried
about their Body weight and it is a V. grate shame
that the media is so obsessed by the way people look
that you just don't see images of ordinary faces any
where. The *only* suitable diet for Teenage Worriers is
a healthy one, including loads of lovely

carbohydrates (bread and pasta and potatoes), loads of lovely vitamins and minerals (fruit and veg), loads of lovely protein (eggs and fish and meat and cheese and nuts and soya beans), loads of lovely variety like rice and pulses and everything yummy. And grate a little fudge on everything if poss.

If **no** Fudge, choccy will do nicely. Slurp.

Dieting also usually doesn't work for a V. V. Simple reason (LISTEN TO THIS BIT AND SHOW IT TO YOUR MUM): When you lose weight, your Body sets off starvation alarm signals and your metabolism slows down. You lose some weight, but it is muscle and water, *not fat*. Meanwhile, your Body gets better at storing what fat it can – because it is Worried it will starve otherwise – so that you actually get *fatter* when you *stop* dieting. This why 95%(ish) of dieters go back to their normal weight within a couple of years. This might sound SCARY, but it isn't – it's reassuring. Your hardworking little (or long or squishy or knobbly) Body is trying to look after you. It has your best interests at heart.

Now forget about food. Except to enjoy it when it's there. Yum, Slurp. More Bigger Fudge Now.

See also EATING DISORDERS.

DISABILITY

If you have a disability you will prob Worry more about everything in this buke than Teenage Worriers who don't. Physical disabilities are bound to make you feel you'll have trouble finding lurve Etck, and it's pretty infuriating to read about stupid Teenage Worriers who are Worrying about their bazooms, spotz Etck if you haven't got a working pair of legs — particularly if you are also spotty and bazoom-free.

I am always V. Surprised how incredibly patient and nice lots of disabled people are, given that I wld want to boot most able-bodied people in the bum if I was them, including *moi*self. Here I am, whingeing on about size of hooter, flappy ears, Etck, and I never stop to think what it wld be like if I couldn't see, or hear, or run. However, everything (even Worrying) is relative and the last thing you want or need if you have disabilities is to be pitied.

One V. Imp fact is to realize you are not ALONE. In fact, one in four people in the UK is either disabled or has a disabled person amongst their family or frendz. Plus, in 1995, there was an act passed by Parliament (The Disability Discrimination Act) which focused on rights for the disabled. Let's hope it starts working soon. So here are a few tips for able-bodied folk:

YES, ONE in FOUR

And how are **WE** today?

Me? Or my Wheels?

Speak to the person, not the wheelchair.

If someone can't see, always say yr own name and the name of the person you're speaking to, so they can follow the conversation.

Don't assume someone with a disability is ill, they're probably healthier than you.

Wise up and don't use horrible thoughtless insults like 'He's spastic' about anyone, disabled or not.

Offer assistance to a disabled Teenage Worrier if you want, but wait for them to accept. (Imagine being propelled over the road when you never wanted to cross it in the first place!)

If you have a disability, chances are you'll already have pals in a similar situation. If not, it's good to join a group so you can share mones and grones. CAMPAIGN for people with disabilities to have the same opportunities as everyone else. Good access for wheelchairs. Use of swimming pools, recreational facilities Etck. And, V. Important, ART. If El Chubb had to condense the most V. Important things to keep MIND and BODY together, they wld probably be the great Outdoors (ie: getting into countryside, or parks) and CREATIVITY (painting, drawing, writing, acting). These are things that will bring happiness to nearly everyone if they are allowed to do them and no-one laughs.

Dreams

There are many bukes and therapies that try to teach you how to remember yr dreams and understand them, one of the most charming of which is to get two pillows, sit on one and pretend the other is your dream. Then you talk to the dream pillow. Later, you sit on the dream pillow and become the dream talking back to you. This sounds sweet and I wld V. Much like to try it, but have sneaking feeling cushion wld turn into giant nightmare-filled beanbag and envelop *moi*.

GCSE options
English
Maths
Daydreaming
Drama
Art
Music
Science

Although I'm sure devoting whole life to study of dreams and their meaning in seething unconscious is V. Noble, I am personally more interested in Daydreams. I have V. Strong desire to put Daydreams on National Curriculum and make it a compulsory GCSE subject for all Teenage Worriers. Why? Cos allowing yrself time to daydream is V. Imp for the soothing of the Soul. Finding time just to let yr thoughts run free may be qu hard in small chaotic households where TV is always blaring, but I find the bath (scented with V. aromatic bubbles Etck) the best place on rare occasions when it is a) unoccupied, and b) hot.

See also MEDITATION.

Drink

Here are a few boozy facts (hic):

Alcohol slows down the brain.

It affects gurlz quicker than boyz.

The lighter you are, the more quickly you're drunk.

One thousand under-15s are admitted to hospital every year with acute alcohol poisoning.

Alcohol is V. Fattening.

Enuf said. And anyway, just the sight of a shandy makes *moi* fall over waving spindly legs in air and singing *I Did It My Way*.

What is IN these pills?

Drugs

Drugs, whether prescribed or not, do work. That is, they affect our delicate systems. We have little receptors all over us that respond to drugs – and one V. Recent theory is that MIND and BODY are so linked that the little information substances (hormones, endorphines, peptides) wander about the Body influencing our cells and therefore how we feel and behave. So our Body is full of natural drugs, and the more we can get them to work, the less we feel in need of other drugs, either for 'recreational' purposes, or even, possibly, for medicinal ones. Exercise, for instance, releases endorphines, which give a natural 'high' and so on.

Obviously, just as people vary in appearance, they also vary in their chemical make-up. Some seem low in serotonin, a neurotransmitter that affects mood (see DEPRESSION), and others low in one or other of the zillions of chemicals that zoom around our little frames. Not surprisingly, this leads many human beans, some of them Teenage Worriers, to seek solace in MIND-altering substances. BUT, argues El Chubb, the more we can tap into our own Inner resources and find all the useful little substances in our own bods, the less likely we are to feel the need for other stuff.

Also, as any true Teenage Worriers knows, there

28

What happened next day....

N.B. The Teenage Worrier on the right tragickly forgot to put on his trousers. Since he also forgot his boxer shorts (and never wears Y fronts) he was expelled... And all because of just one night in the embrace of Cruella de Drugge...

is no way of knowing what is in the tab of E or whatever you might be tempted by, so FEAR is a good reason to steer clear. I reckon they'll legalize cannabis (which loads of people smoke and believe does V. little harm) one of these days, which at least will mean father can't be retrospectively arrested, but fear of Breaking the Law and getting arrested, fined or even jailed is enuf for *moi* to steer clear. My real fear, though, is of going really MAD as a result of drugges, cos I have seen it happen.

Also, if you feel under pressure cos it seems everyone is doing it, take comfort from the fact that this just isn't true. Latest statistics in 14–16-yr-old age group show that 30% have tried illegal drugs. This means that 70% haven't! Also, many of the 30% will only have tried something once. More disconcertingly, by the age of 22, 90% of Teenage Worriers will have been offered illegal drugges. So learning to say 'no' is werth practising.

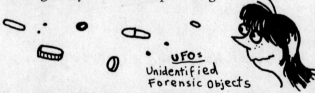

UFOs
Unidentified
Forensic Objects

NB Heroin now V. Easily available. Do not be persuaded that chasing dragon will turn you into Train-Spotting heroin(e), however. It will not only cost you arm and leg but V. Likely life – or else life-long misery of addiction.

EATING DISORDERS

Eating disorders like *anorexia*, where the sufferer starves themselves and believes they are fat even when they're painfully thin, and *bulimia*, where the sufferer alternately starves and binges, emptying the contents of the fridge into gob and then deliberately making themselves throw up, are on the increase. If you are genuinely overweight and also very tired, you could have a thyroid disorder and it is simple to check this with a blood test.

Warning signs to look out for **in Eating Disorders**:
* An obsession with food, but a reluctance to eat.
* Not liking to share meals with other people – and leaving the table early.
* Secretive behaviour.
* Frequent self-weighing.
* And, obviously, loss of weight.

Although it sound as though these disorders are self-inflicted and therefore deserve no under-standing, they are in fact *very dangerous* and it is important to get medical and psychological help as soon as possible. In so far as the reasons for them are known, they seem to do with being over-stressed and worried and trying to get control over just one thing in yr life.

See also SELF-HARM.

Erogenous Zones

Erogenous Zones are mainly supposed to be just the Naughty Bits . . . but for Teenage Worriers all zones are erogenous if fondled – or even sensuously skimmed – by the Right Person. I am V. Disappointed the Erogenous is not included among the Zones you can visit on a one-day Travelcard.

Travel card? Which zone?

Erogenous

But not All the way...

I think the Govt should declare a few square miles of each city to be an erogenous zone, where people can parade about canoodling Etck with no fear of harassment, wearing exactly what they like and doing nothing but ROMANTIC stuff. Cameras and professional hookers wld have to be excluded, as this would all be for free. Sigh.

Exercise

What middle-aged Worriers do to work off excesses of their yoof. Teenage Worriers shld be nicely toned anyway and I find walking into our apology of a sitting room and turning on the TV (if I can find it amid the piles of DIY magazines, Lego and tubes of oil paint left by my revolting family) quite enough exercise thank you V. Much. However, this is a responsible tome so I shld stress that exercise is V. Imp if you want to feel healthy in MIND and BODY.

If you get to like your bod and feed it nice nourishing stuff and exercise it, it will wag its tail at you. Fat dogs don't get enough exercise. How many people are mean enough not to exercise their dogs? But we're too mean to exercise ourselves, viz: be sure to walk upstairs rather than take a lift Etck (unless you are in the top floor of a tower block, in which case it wld be V. tiring) or in a house (in which case it wld be V. Unlikely you wld have a lift). Actually,

I'm not sure when this advice is supposed to apply, so I will move on to next thing, which is:

EL CHUBB'S EXERCISE TIPS
Consider the following:
1) Walk to school if poss, swing arms in merry fashion. Sometimes, run.
b) If near river, row to school (rowing exercises all of you at once, and with V. Little effort).
3) Consider joining in organized stuff at school a bit more. Why not actually climb that rope instead of staring glumily at it as though it is a dinosaur neck from dume?
D) How about actually, er, joining in with OTHER people (Radical!). Table tennis is V. Good if you have just one frend, but if you have more than one, team games can be a larf.
e) Dance!
f) Yoga! (V. gentle, spirichual Etck.)
7) Wild Nookie (chance wld be fine thing).
8) Hide channel-changer and walk to TV set.

Exhausting toe exercise

Eyes

Windows to soul. Huh. If
this were true then I wd
be living with Adam
Stone in eternal bliss, cos
his eyes definitely said I
lurve you for ever and
then he bunked off to Los Angeles . . .

Fantasy

I have a big prob distinguishing between Fantasy
and Reality, partly because I spend much more of
my time doing the former than living in the latter. I
used to fantasize about winning the Grand National,
Horse of the Year Show Etck, then had V. Brief
period of knowing I wld be V. Famous model (ho
ho). Now I know I will become V. World-famous
Film Director (this will actually happen, so doesn't
count as Fantasy). But I waste hours inventing
scenarios about exactly what Adam and I will say to
each other when we are looking back on our loooong
happy relationship, and all over the Western Werld
there are Teenage Worriers fantasizing about what
they will say when Leonardo di Yum Yum turns his
dazzling orbs towards their Kate Winsome-style

36

tressess . . . sigh . . . and so it goes on . . . and on.

I suppose, once you are on the roller-coaster of Fantasy you never get off. Though I am sure that when my lurve is requited, I will be able to concentrate my LIFE energies on Film Directing and use my powers of Fantasy to help mankind with V. Moving Imaginative documentaries about Human Suffering Etck.

FENG SHUI

Hey, wow, you can tone up yr room! This ancient Chinese Art sez: make yr environment happy to make yr self happy. It sez that each area of the house you live in represents a different area of yr life – and then goes on to say scary things like, if your loo is in your wealth area then you're prob flushing all dosh down toilet. This is obviously true in Chubb household. NB Feng Shui cure for this is always keeping loo seat down. (I imagine they mean while yr not using it . . .)

HAPPY RUME

GLUMEY RUME

Atmosphere is in YOUR hands....

Teenage Worriers are, of course, helpless victims of their parents when it comes to houses: ie: we have V. Little control over whether we live in neat tidy flat or tousled mansion, Etck. But you might try a little Feng Shui in yr own bedrume, involving mirrors, little silver balls, crystals, jolly plants Etck.

NB Tell yr folks that, according to Feng Shui, yr front door and hall are V. Imp. Make em as nice, light, clutter-free Etck as poss. Arg, brief survey of hall at current moment reveals:

On floor: Two pairs trainers, four other shoes (not matching), one Wellington boot, eighteen leaflets for pizzas, nine leaflets for double-glazing, sixteen circulars, three cards from postman asking parents to collect unpaid-for mail, Rover's toy mouse, nasty rotten green thing that may be ancient tangerine, four little plastic figures, two toy cars, a kite, a ping-pong bat, last year's Christmas *Beano*, a bicycle pump, lots of fluff (it's quite tidy just now).
On wall: Two hooks, astonishingly supporting fifteen garments that resemble jackets, five scarves, a broken umbrella and three baseball caps.

GARDENS

Getting back to soil where we all come from and to which we must one day return (sigh) is obviously a V. Deep and meaningful soulful experience for many.

I have been somewhat disappointed in gardening attempts, possibly due to small concrete yard, but I do not deny that the joy of seeing tiny shoot emerging, heralding Spring, changing seasons etck can be V. Rewarding and it is my ambition to get Granny Chubb a little patch of Earth one day in which to exercise her remarkable green fingers (even her fish fingers are green, ha ha yeeech).

Seed tended by Moi

Seed tended by
Granny Chubb

What she does with a window-box should be at the Chelsea Flower Show. *Moi* thinks spending some time growing things is V. Creative and good for soul, espesh if it's nice herbs to flavour the fish fingers Etck.

GLUMES

Rear their horrible chasms over:
1) Undone schoolwork.
2) Undone buttons (which you notice when you have been one hour on tube with everyone laughing at yr underwear).
3) Domestic catastrophe, eg: terminal illness, fatal accident, divorce Etck. If you experience any of these in yr teenage years you will understand how V. superficial are the other glumes mentioned above. But everything is relative, so they say.

See also DEPRESSION.

Habits

BURP Hic Right! Knowot I mean?

People often don't tell
you about Yr Bad Habits
to be kind, but I think it
is a mark of a True Friend that they do. To judge by
Adored Parents, Granny Chubb Etck, habits that are
quite unnoticeable in Yoof can become V.
Maddening and Conspicuous as you get older and
care less and less what anybody thinks, so it wld be
good to try to zap them early on.

Habitz that tend to revolt others are: loud farting
followed by louder larfter (as though you think it V.
Clever to fart); overt nose-picking involving
examination of yr bogeys; saying 'Right' or 'D'You
know what I mean' after every three werds.

My own Habits include: obsession with even
numbers which leads to *moi* wanting to touch
everything twice; biting nails to kwick and therefore
never cultivating Cruella de Ville style talons;
twisting my fringe around my finger, which leads to
finger becoming V. Tangled in knots of wig;
carrying lucky rabbit's foot (animal-lovers note: not
real rabbit's foot) at all times; kissing pictures of my
family before I go to sleep; praying at all times in
unlikely situations.

The above all embarrass *moi*, but are not too
harmful to anyone else (I think).

Happiness

A V. Famous Person of Eng Lit (W. H. Auden, who wrote the V. Sad poem in *Four Weddings and a Funeral*) said that we have a Duty to Be Happy. This seems to *moi* to be one of the more interesting thingz that Persons of Eng Lit have said about how we should all carry on.

The Happiest Person I Know is Granny Chubb. She's kind to everybody, has fun doing V. Simple things she's done for years, and doesn't yearn for things she'll never have. I can't work out if this is because the Game of Life has slowed down as far as she's concerned, and she's just given up (having high expectations of anything is, of course, a bit of waste of time in our family anyway) or because she's always been a Zen Buddhist disguised with a pac-a-mac and a Tesco bag, and her Needs Are Few. I think the real reason is that she's delighted with anything that turns up to make her Happy, has been putting on a Happy Vibe as a bit of a duty to those around her for so long it became second nature, and is open to Happiness but doesn't expect some strange Elixir called Happiness out of Life as a Right. She is a Model to *moi*, though maybe you can only get to behave like that by being Old.

Granny
Chubb

Hot
Water
Bottle

HOT CHOCCY

Rover, fleas
and all

Yes!
FUDGE!

V.Gude
Buke
by
Ivan
Idear

Just a sprinkling of the AVAILABLE (as
opposed to unavailable, sob....) things that make
MOI happy....

Health

Ever had one of those weeks (months, years . . .) where everything seems to go wrong and you feel like doing nothing but groning soulfully under duvet or gazing tragickly at rain dripping down glumey window Etck? And THEN you get flu, complete with exploding head, throbbing eyelids, graveyard wheeze, suppurating hooter — and you realize that compared to this you have been feeling just great?

Just a small sample of supplies I like to carry if I'm away for more than a couple of hours.

It is at times like this that the av Teenage Worrier promises never to complain about anything ever again if they can only just feel well. Although this is usually a short-lived promise, it is werth remembering that good health is one of ye grate gifts of life and werth hanging on to at all costs.

Herbs

V. Ancient remedies for a
zillion ills can be found growing
in the gardens of our once grate
nation – but understanding them wld
take a herbal encyclopaedia. I am V. Fond
of herbs and spices on food Etck . . . so by all
means add a little rosemary and tarragon to yr
chips or fudge.

V. strange-but-true Fact that while Rosemary and
Basil are names for herbs *and* people, Tarragon and
Coriander are not. It is werthless but charming
thoughts such as these that provide much solace for
*moi*self.

Hips

Sexiest bit of bod in Adam's case. Strong Sekshul
connotations generally, due to muscular
requirements involved in Doing It, Giving Birth
Etck. Hip movements in dancing Etck thus often
targeted by V. Bossy People in Olden Times (1950s)
as signs of moral decline in Teenagers. Must admit
however the El Chubb attempts at dirty dancing
look like stick insect suddenly discovering it has
taken up residence on bonfire.

45

Homeopathy

Our own noble Royal Family believes in
Homeopathy, which enables them to live to Great
Ages and thus have even more time for being
dysfunctional, shooting wildlife, shaking hands with
baffled passers-by Etck. Homeopathy is treating like
with like, which means giving you a bit of the
disease so you don't catch the full unedited version.
On this basis, Ickle Benjy is obviously a
Homeopathist, because when he gets a cold he blows
V. tiny missiles of snot out of his V. tiny nostrils at
moi, but it hasn't worked so far because it always
gives me the worst cold in the history of the
Yuniverse, even prob including people who live on
some really cold and miserable place like Uranus,
pardon me.

Homeopathy was invented by a German doc
called Hahnemann, who thought docs were all

46

wrong to splash medicines all over the place by the bucketful, and they worked best in V. tiny quantities. This came as welcome news to patients in the 18th and 19th centuries, when Hahnemann was at work, because it was a lot better than having leeches stuck all over yr Bod. It comes as less welcome news to the Western drugs industry in the 20th century, which wants us all to use large quantities of the stuff they make. Homeopathy has been shown to be V. useful in some conditions that can't be fixed in other ways, like allergies Etck, and many people believe in it because it isn't filling yr Bod with dodgy chemicals that may have long-term side effects.

Hormones

These are chemical substances produced by an endocrine gland and transported in the bludde to certain tissues, on which they have an amazing effect (eg: on boyz' willies Etck). There are loads of hormones buzzing around inside Teenage Worriers, once they start developing sexually. These busy little substances are what make you get urges, cause mood swings, periods, spots as well as Body hair, bazooms and bigger willies. Still, although the little fiends often make us filled with glume, we are better off with them. Cos no hormones = No SEX. Also no HUMAN RACE.

Don't be scared!

Hormones of a Teenage Worrier

IMAGE

Er, THINK (I know it hurts that brain cell) about all that junk in magazines like *Weeny-bop*, *Smirk* Etck that tells you to what to wear, how to do your wig, how much food, exercise Etck Etck you shld be having. What are they saying it FOR? At least with El Chubb's pearls of wisdom you know that she is doing it from the painful experience of a fellow Worrier in the vineyards of Glume. But *Smirk* is just trying to sell more advertising, T-shirts, gunk Etck.

Everybody Worries about their image and poses a bit, say I. If we didn't care at all what people thought of us, we wld prob be V. Arrogant or V. Saintly. Teenage Worriers *have* to do a lot of Posing, it is part of Finding Out Who We Are. It goes like this: dress up in old Tesco's bags held together with Christmas sellotape and boots discarded by giant gas-fitter and found on skip, smear wig with motor oil, stick Granny Chubb hatpin through left eyebrow, hang out singing shouting-song at top of voice. This will divide Werld into those who tell you to Jump Under Bus and those who purr 'wicked' and try to slide hand into Tesco bag.

If you like the people who tell you to Jump Under Bus and don't like the hand-sliders, you have Found Out Something About yerself, and can try another Pose. Eventually you will find a Pose that makes you feel comfortable with Yrself, and Happy with those you like. Later, of course, when you apply for Job in Bank, or Lawyers' Office, or supermarket checkout, you realize you have to start another Pose to stand any chance of Success. This pose is smiling a lot and saying 'No Prob'. If this Pose fits perfectly with yr Inner Nature, you are V. Blessed and Fortunate Person and not at all like *moi*.

JOSS STICKS

Nice smelly things that look like those little bits of rafia you used to do weaving with at nursery skule. Instead, you light these and lie back to inhale gorgeous perfume. Often used, according to my only father, to disguise smells of illegal drugges way back in the 70s.

KARMA

According to Hindus and Buddhists, this is about all the things you do in this life that will affect you both in this life and in your next life. Hence, doing something bad is avoided because it's bad karma, Etck. Some folks claim to be able to tell if you've got good karma or not just by looking at you. When I look at Syd Snoggs in Year Ten, I think I see what they mean. Arg.

Leonardo da Vinci

Fabulous before-his-time maęstro of Science and Art, who united MIND and BODY in incredible drawings of people, pants *(shouldn't that be plants? – Ed)*, water and machines. His most famous pic is the Moaner *(Shouldn't that be Mona? – Ed)* Lisa, but he also drew flying machines centuries before they existed and wrote in mirror-writing in his incredible journals about many things, including the great beauty of the human face at dusk, when the dying light illumines its softness. Ahhhhhhh. I include him, cos it can be V. Inspiring to look at werk of genius and feel amazed that someone with exactly same number of heads, arms, legs, eyes Etck as you cld actually do all that stuff. This shld not make you feel werthless worm by comparison, but give you sense of pride in the grate potential of humanity, ie: that is YOU.

Make-up

Argh. El Chubb's attempt to find perfect stretch-over-yr-own-to-wear-at-parties FACE has so far failed. Even if you could get a really good one, what wd be the point, since no-one wd know who you were the next day and Prince Charming might not

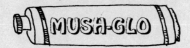

fancy running around with rubber mask saying find
the gurl who fits this? Or maybe he would – in
which case you'd prob run a mile . . .

In the absence of the
ready-to-wear FACE, I
have often dreamt of a
perfect make-up you cld
just roll on that would
do lips, eyes, and rest of
mug in one fell swoop
instead of having to buy
all those dinky little
tubes and cylinders and
packets and then having
to get a little make-up
bag that they can all leak
out onto. Naturally, ahem, in a spiritual buke such
as this, one shld be concentrating on higher things,
but now that seven-year-olds are painting their
nails, it is V. Hard to resist blandishments of make-
up ads, with their freshly glowing, glossy-lipped,
shining-eyed, healthy-looking gurlz all grinning out
at you from every page . . . Resist it if you can,
however, and rely, as I do (hollow laughter, sounds
of fingers crossing) on attaining true inner beauty by
thinking good thoughts, eating good food and
breathing good lungfuls of good fresh air (arg,
choke, asthma Etck).

If this fails, get V. Cheap stuff not tested on
animals.

Just add
scowl

MEDITATION

Both Only Mother and Adored Father have
occasionally gone in for Meditation, to contact their
Inner Selves, and try to discover if it's possible to
share a house with Floor-phobic infants, bazoomless
Teenage Worriers, bathroom-monopolizing
Romeos, psychotic gerbils, embittered cats, and
Each Other without being dragged away to Ye
Binne.

In Only Mother's case,
this has involved locking
herself in the bedroom at
dawn and sitting cross-
legged on a blanket,
going *OMMMMM* until
finally surrendering to
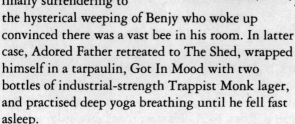
the hysterical weeping of Benjy who woke up
convinced there was a vast bee in his room. In latter
case, Adored Father retreated to The Shed, wrapped
himself in a tarpaulin, Got In Mood with two
bottles of industrial-strength Trappist Monk lager,
and practised deep yoga breathing until he fell fast
asleep.

Adored Mother became anxious after a while, searched high and low (including Shed, where she overlooked gently undulating tarpaulined heap in corner) and finally called Ye Bill. Meditating Father finally awoke to find family of woodlice occupying trouser-pockets and stumbled indoors to combined Fury of Only Mother and Vast Policemen issuing All Points Bulletins into radios.

Both of these circs, of course, are stressful enough to need about twice as much meditation to cure the effects as the meditation that started it all in the first place. But many people *do* meditate without these mishaps (it is just a question of finding the right place and time), and research has proved that it can reduce stress, improve the chemical balances in yr Bod, and enhance health. You can either meditate using one of the prescribed methods – there are Transcendental Meditation centres all over the country, and those studying yoga use a series of deep-breathing and focusing exercises to help meditation – or practise simpler, non-religious methods like Mindfulness. Mindfulness was invented by American biologist Prof Kabat-Zinn (it's true, it's true) and is similar to yoga in getting you to listen to yrself rather than constantly thinking of doing something, or Worrying about something you haven't done.

OOм м м м м м м м м м м м м м м

NATURE

Even in ye most blissful countryside there is
usually one who feels ALONE.

One of the greatest soothers for MIND and BODY
is to amble amid waving corn, gazing at fluffy
clouds, with only the sounds of fluffy lambs and the
chirrupping melodies of twinkly birdies for
company, Aaaaaah Meeeeee! Harrrumph, I can hear
the myriad voices of country-dwelling Teenage
Worriers who are forced to stumble about on bleak
moorlands waiting for the one bus every other
month.

You Teenage Worriers who live in the country see us townies as mindless zealots who get all the fun and then tell you off for maiming foxes and breeding mad cows Etck. This is V. True and V. Unfair, especially since townies get all V. Soppy about countryside, just as I do . . . and only use it to waft about in without giving a thought as to what it's actually like to live there. Fact is, country folk have rubbish transport and are often living far from all the stuff we take for granted. (Klubs! Shops! Cinemas! Kulchure! Frendz!)

So, El Chubb's advice for town-dwelling Teenage Worriers is, if you want a complete change, spend a week in the country. And for country-dwelling Teenage Worriers if YOU want a complete change, spend a week in the town. Maybe two weeks is better . . . Everyone will be V. Happy, feel refreshed and stimulated in MIND and BODY and will be V. Happy to return to their own nachural habitat. Er, maybe . . .

OILS

Say YES to Oils and Unguents. Massage them deeply into your knobbly or billowy bod. Roll in them! You can heat them for nice smells, add them to your nosh (er, olive oil Etck, not aromatherapy oils) and know that oil is oiling yourself inside and out. You NEED oil!

Panics

ARGHHH!

Panics, phobias Etck rule our lives more than we know. We all have little compulsions that we keep secret from everybody else (and if you don't have any, you are V. Lucky). To be as scared of floors as my ickle brother Benjy is, though, is to be too scared. I sometimes Worry that maybe he is secretly aiming to be one of those kids who are forced to live in a bubble, as he wants Tabloid newspaper readers to send him teddies Etck. His phobias are not helped by endless Worry heaped on him by my guilty mother. She is sure that he suffers from being youngest, suffers from looking V. Cute and therefore not being taken seriously, suffers from dyslexia Etck. If Benjy is dyslexic then I am mashed otatop, but the middle classes all seem to assume that their boyz are dyslexic if they are not reading Dickens Etck at five, and clearly my only Mother is keen to continue thinking of herself as a toff, despite all financial indications to the contrary.

However, if you feel as engulfed by Worries as Benjy, and that your phobias or weird habitz are a little bit TOO weird and are stopping you living Normal Life (whatever that is) then do go to doc. They will not think you are mad, but they really can provide help for these things, to avoid you ending up like Jack Nicholson in *As Good As It Gets*.

PERIODS

I have writ much about ye periods in my many other tomes, so I have only this to add: Be V. V. Nice to yrself if you have V. Bad periods. Wear long warm tights, take long warm baths, take long warm drinks, snuggle up to long warm boyz (I mean, sofas) and, if poss, strap long warm hot-water bottle to yr middle at all times.

Since Bad Moods often precede Bad periods, you shld start this process a week before yr period is due and continue a week after for comfort's sake. This shld leave you free for one week a month to be 'normal'. Only joking. Honest, this is the kind of advice they used to give gurlz, including things like not swimming and all that. But most of us feel fine during periods. If you don't, see doc. There are V. Good things to help with V. heavy bleeding and cramps these daze.

PRIVACY

Teenage Worriers need privacy. Demand locks on all doors, especially bathroom (ours is always broken and I can hardly sit on loo for five seconds without Benjy barging in waving sting ray lazer gun Etck). Parents go on and on about their privacy but seem to think my life shld be open buke, ie: 'Who was that on phone? What did they want? Where are you going? Look at state of yr wig!' Etck. If I talked to them like that they wld go up wall.

QUALITY OF LIFE

This whole buke is supposed to be about Quality of Life. We all have a Fantastic quality of Life if we compare ourselves to cave persons, or even to Roman Emperors Etck. They did not have TVs, telephones, fridges, blah blah. But there is no definite answer as to whether they were happier or more serene than us.

What you can bet on, however, is that the poor have always envied the rich. El Chubb believes that *Quality* of Life equals *Equality* of life, and will only be achieved when all of us — the clever and the stoopid, even the V. V. lazy — have enuf security to feel dignified and part of society Etck. Until this golden daye, we will suffer either envy cos we haven't got stuff or guilt cos we have. Whichever category you fit in, you know in yr soul that peace of MIND and BODY is what you're after. So CAMPAIGN to change werld Etck, but also to change self and enjoy the fleeting moment.

RELIGION

The subject of Religion is one that causes considerable confusion to *moi*. As a Teenage Worrier I have, naturally, a V. strong desire for Higher

Power to exist. But also as a Teenage Worrier, I sometimes harbour fears that He, She or It may not. This wld be sadder than finding out there's no tooth fairy.

If you have a belief that enables you to stop wasting time Worrying about the Vast Abyss Beyond and get on with Life and Lurve, it's a V. Good Thing. But beware: if you have a belief that's V. Critical of anything and everybody then it isn't Good, say I. I must say I have a pref. for Religions which are Tolerant and Peaceful and that say being a Yuman Being is a Good Thing and not a Lifelong Disaster only cured by Banana, Purging In Fires of Hell Etck.

I espech like the sound of some kinds of Buddhism (Ommmmmmmmmmmm) because it seems to *moi* that it can be a way of bringing Yr Bod and Yr Minde into Harmony, though in the case of the Bod of El Chubb the two might be better off keeping well away from each other. But the nice thing about Religions that encourage Meditation and tuning in to Yr Bod's energies Etck, is that they maybe help you to Live more fully in the Moment Yr Akshully In, rather than biting yr nails about something you did or didn't do in The Past, or might or might not do in The Future, and they can be V. Calming. It is also possible to smuggle these things into Yr Everyday Life without drawing attention to them, rather than with more finger-wagging religions that oblige you to look like

NOT IMPOSSIBLE that bicycles orbit in space...

BUT V.V. Unlikely

Florence Nightingale, or go around with a V. Understanding Maddening Espesh Quiet Voice, or a sandwich board saying in big letters RELIGIOUS PERSON.

They say the more Partickle Physicists Etck find out about all the whizzing, orbiting, colliding things that make the Universe work, the more Religious they get. I'm not surprised. If I spend every day proving that everything in my Life from Adored Father and Mother to Horace are really empty space joined together by flying Bitz and Pieces, I'd need as much Religion as I could get to relieve the Worry of why they don't all fly off in a million different directions and hit the wall. (But of course the wall is a kazillion flying thingz too, aaargh . . .)

RITUALS

MIND and BODY are both soothed by all kinds of Rituals, from religious ones (see above) to comforting ones like always having a hot bath, or a mug of hot choccy Etck. Benjy has about two hundred and twenty little things he has to do at bedtime. I've got mine down to about four . . .

Self-defence

All Teenage Worriers, whether boyz or gurlz, have fear of being jumped on or beaten up in street. Although learning ancient arts of self-defence such as judo, karate Etck cld help to improve yr confidence, they are not infallible, espesh if jumped on by horde of lethal weapon-wielding thugs. No-one can guarantee complete safety, wherever they live, so it is worth bearing in MIND a few simple hints and sticking to them:

* If poss, stick with someone you know when out after dark.
* Don't get drawn into conversations with strangers, just cos you're embarrassed about seeming rude.
* Only carry the dosh that you need for that day/evening.
* Keep to brightly lit, familiar streets.
* Tell your folks/caring adult where you're going and arrange a time to be back by.
* Any hint of an attack, just run like hell.
* If you can't run, just kick, bite and scream for help really loudly.

LONELY MOOR

In films, heroines are always wandering about on above. DO NOT follow their example.

SELF-HARM

If you do this you R NOT alone

It is a V. Sad fact that many Teenage Worriers commit acts of self-harm, such as cutting or burning themselves. Usually, this is done in private and the Teenage Worrier thinks he/she is the only person in the world who is doing such things. It is incredibly important, if you are driven to injure yourself, to try to find help from sympathetic people. There are organizations devoted to helping people who self-harm and who are very clear about getting rid of the myths surrounding it, like it's 'just attention-seeking', or 'It's self-inflicted so it's not serious', or 'If you won't see the psychiatrist you can't want to get better'.

These organizations will not tell you any of the above, but instead will try to understand your particular needs – so if you or a frend are self-harming, get in touch. (See numbers at end of buke.) You will feel less alone and may be able to begin to unravel the reasons why you self-harm – which are obviously different for each individual.

SMOKING

Hey, wow, here's something that smells like barbecued underpants, costs about half what a pensioner has to live on and KILLS you. Buy now!

Fag advertising is actually looking more and more like the above, now that every ad has a warning notice – but obviously Teenage Worriers are attracted to danger, excitement Etck and so even if you plastered the message 'Don't buy, this is timed to kill you, personally, in two minutes' over every pack, it might still not put Teenage Worriers off. A visit to a lung cancer ward might. So might the sight of all the dosh you're going to spend on smoking going up in flames before you. Cos it's true, once you start, it's incredibly difficult to stop (look at my own dear parents). But you know this already . . . Trouble is, Teenage Worriers have many yearnings and if you have V. Deep desire to take V. Harmful substances, you could just be a bit low in energy. Worth indulging in the many nice things to make yr bod feel nice and lurved and cherished that I am advising in this buke and put off smoking until you're thirty. By then, you'll prob be fine without it.

Trouble is, V. SCARY pix like this, ENCOURAGE some of us...

PS: Try kissing an ashtray some time and think what the boy/gurl of yr dreams wd think if *your* breath smelt like that.

SNOW-SAUNA

Snow is just frozen rain, but it seems like a lot more than that. Because it is made of V. Pretty crystals (and not a single snowflake is exactly like any other one, which is a V. Nice Wonders-of-Nachur thought) and it completely changes the familiar werld outside your door so you wake up in the morning and everything looks like picture postcard, children's story Etck, it is one of those magical thingz that is amazing because it's a surprise.

Benjy always hopes it will Snow, espesh at Christmas, but in his little LIFE he has so far hardly ever seen any, and what he has seen turns into stuff that looks like thick mushy carpet of snot pretty quickly. I also remember (though he, fortunately, has forgotten) that in the winter in which he first learned to walk it did Snow, and he went straight out and sank up to his knees in it. Adored Parents clapped hands with glee like in Dick Van Dyke films, laughed at him, took pix Etck, while he wailed piteously and looked like kitten dropped into puddle. This may have been the root of Benjy's prob, we think.

I also remember Adored Father witnessing unexpected blizzard whilst drunk and in the midst of unpredictable mood swings due to ongoing relationship with Trapeze Artist, and flinging off all clothes, plunging into skin-peeling hot bath and then running out to roll around in snow-filled yard, emitting strange chants Etck. He later insisted that this was simply much cheaper than visiting a sauna, and Blessed By Nature anyway, but I think it was the point at which Adored Mother began to suspect something was up with him. So you can see El Chubb looks on the arrival of Snow with mixed feelings. Nonetheless, I will V. Definitely try the snow-sauna on first possible occasion, as long as it is night and the neighbours can't see.

STAR SIGNS

As you know, El Chubb is V. Cynical about horoscopes Etck which does not stop *moi* from reading *ROMANCE in the Stars — the Guide to your purrfect partner* every time they print the same article in *Weenybop*.

A V. New & Exciting STAR SIGN has been discovered: <u>PEGAMARUS</u>. It is a mix of Air and Water and if you are lucky enough to be born under it you will have ability to fly.
(N.B. Don't try this at home).

As a Taurean, I'm supposed to get on well with other Earth signs (Virgo and Capricorn) and have deep and fatal attractions to Scorpios, Sagittarians Etck. How do I know all this if I don't believe a werd of it? Because most Teenage Worriers do. It's part of yoof kulchure among gurlz to drool over horoscopes and even to believe crazed women who write the future in Teen magazines.

NB If you want to prove you can guess someone's Star sign try El Chubb's proven method:

V. Thin person: Libra.

Redhead: Capricorn.

Tearful: Aquarius.

Wearing pink jumper: certainly a Gemini.

Freckles and lop-sided grin: Scorpio

Very short legs with small lumpy feet: Aries

As you see, the above is all B*ll*cks.

NB2 One of my frendz' mums takes all this very seriously and has her own personal astrologer (gulp). I suppose if you spend a lifetime studying it, there might be something in it, but it wd have to be V. personal and not from magazines . . .

SWIMMING WITH DOLPHINS

I bet not a single Teenage Worrier reading this buke has akshully swum with a dolphin – and yet, and yet . . . You wld all like to, wouldn't you? This is one of those fantasies everyone has, of humanity at one with the animals Etck, and we also have V. Nice impression of dolphins with their V. Big brains (bigger than ours) and smiley faces.

Recently there was a story of an eight-year-old boy who had never spoken. His Mum somehow scraped together £10,000 to send him for three weeks to a therapy centre in the USA and he spoke his first word after swimming with dolphins! Phew. Even ye most cynical reader will swune with pleasure at this thought and immediately demand that dolphin-swimming be included on ye National Curriculum. Dolphins shld clearly be in charge of all skules, prisons, remand homes Etck.

If only Prime Ministers, Head teachers, Etck looked more like this

Pause for a moment while reading, dear Teenage Worrier, and imagine you are diving deep into crystal waters with yr dolphin buddy, only to swoop up again in a cloud of shimmering spray twinkling in sunbeams. Sigh.

NB It is worth imagining this while you are swimming . . . Not qu. as good as Real Thing, but V. Soothing all the same. AND, if you *have* swum with dolphins, write in to El Chubb, I wld love to hear about it.

T'AI CHI

T'Ai Chi is an ancient Chinese martial art in which you don't do anything martial, ie: you don't actually kick anybody, except by accident.

It's mentioned in a V. Old buke, the *I Ching* or *Buke of Changes*, and comes from the Chinese meaning 'Great Ultimate'. It's supposed to unite Yin and Yang, the passive and active forces in Ye Universe. Now, El Chubb has seen people practising T'ai Chi, which involves a lot of standing on one leg, weaving around like revolving figure in musical box, and usually falling over, and it doesn't look all that Ultimate to me, except maybe the Ultimate Humiliation. However, the path to yr Spiritual Essence is a long one and requires patience, and anything you do as regular exercise, and to put you in better tune with Yr Bod can only be a Good Thing.

73

UFOS

Vast numbers of people on planet believe in UFOs and, if UFO stood for Unidentified Fallen Object, so wld I, as our floors are littered with them. Hmmmmm . . . little green bit of plastic with knobbly purple attachment. What can it be? Maybe it's from other Werld? Etck.

I am V. Suspicious of tales of invaders from Outer
Space whisking yuman beans away for experiments,
however, which seem to be all the rage in the U.S.A.
Doubtless, among the zillions of galaxies that we
can't even see, there are likely to be other little
creatures rather like ourselves, but so far they are
keeping V. Quiet, prob because, like us, they
haven't invented anything that travels faster than
speed of light. V. Exciting though, to hear there is
water on the moon. This means there might well
have been life on Moon . . . gasp. Have never quite
understood why scientists assume that life needs
oxygen, water, Etck. You'd think there must be
forms of life that have learnt to live by breathing
stuff we wld find noxious. And I am not talking
about Benjy lying under his covers smelling farts.

VEGETARIANISM

There have been so many food scares recently that a
lot of Teenage Worriers have become V. V. Worried
about what they eat, leading to an increase in Eating
Disorders or just general pickiness. Many Teenage
Worriers are turning to vegetarianism as a more
healthy and ethical way of noshing. But it's only
healthy if you eat enough protein. Campaigning for
organic, free range meat is also a good option. The
animals have a nice life as well as a nicer taste.

Voice

Dum-di-dum, tarradiddle, tiddley widdly tra la laaaaaaaa.

Singing makes you Happy says Professor L. Chubb,
author of 'BIRDS DON'T GET DEPRESSED'.

When you were a little pre-Teenage Worrier, toddling around yr nursery, you didn't Worry how you sounded, or what noise you made, did you? You cried when you were hurt or sad, you bellowed when you were angry, you laughed like drain when jolly and you SANG. As we get older, sadder, wiser, bogged down with life's adversity Etck, these sounds become controlled and we do, quite literally, 'lose our voice'. El Chubb believes that singing makes you happy. Try it. Just utter a few bouncy notes when feeling low, or hum in the bath. Pay no attention to horrible family saying you can't sing in tune Etck.

Waist

V. Imp for joining berm to top of bod. Try to forget about it otherwise as it is not vis in most Teen Worriers (most will be straight-up-and-down like *moi*, or spherical like my frend Aggy. My other frend, Hazel, moan whinge envy, is unique exception). Waists only used to be teeny in the days of my namesake Scarlett O'Hara when whalebone corsets were used to squeeze waists up into bosoms and down into hips. This was before conservationists stepped in on behalf of whales, thereby doing females V. Good turn and ensuring they started getting good GCSEs instead of fainting in coils.

XTENSIONS (HAIR, WILLY)

Boyz get even more Worried about their willies than gurlz do about their bazooms. And who can blame them? Your bazooms just have to hang about – if you are lucky enough to have something that actually can hang – whereas ye willy has to go up and down, in and out and often does all this with no instruction whatever from its owner and at wrong moments, like when shaking hands with your Mum's boss and glimpsing picture of Sharon Grone over his shoulder Etck.

As for SIZE – well, a 12-year-old boy'z willy is usually between about 3 and 5cm whereas an adult's is between 6 and

V. Small (or big) willy within

10cm when dormant and between 12 and 19cm (4 to 7 inches) when rampant. Now you know. Does this help? Are you likely to go around with a measuring tape to check out your lurved one's tackle? Is he likely to? If so, make sure he's careful it's not one of those steel retractable ones that whip back and arrrrrg.

Same goes for bazooms. You've either got them or not, and if you are V. V. Worried about extending same you shld ask yrself why. I did, and the answer I gave *moi*self was: I'd like to have bigger ones, please.

Still, I know I won't have silicone implants Etck. I don't like the idea of all that stuff floating around or poss leaking out. And what wld I be doing it FOR? (To get bigger ones.) There are more important things in life (yes, but what?). Seriously, you know there are.

Of course, extending yr wig is a far simpler matter and good harmless fun. Unless wig is like my own, and breaks into electric frizz at sight of hairpin.

YAWNING

Ever noticed how V. Contagious yawning is? If you Yawn on a bus, ten to one you will notice someone else has caught it. It is grate fun doing this with a frend; Hazel and I once got a whole tube carriage yawning together. While engaging in this harmless merry prank you can congratulate yrself on how good it is for everyone to Yawn. It is a V. Good release of pressure, since lots of tension, apparently, is in our necks and jaws. Yawning lets it out. CAMPAIGN now for more yawning!

Just looking at these pics shld. make you YAWN

YOGA

Omm di om di om di di om
Om di-om-di-om-dee dee
om

Both Only Mother and Adored Father have
attempted Yoga at various times. Adored Father
even went to a class for a while – until (according to
one of Ashley's girlfriends, whose mum went to the
same class) the dreaded yoga farting phenomenon set
him for ever on the lonely path to Higher
Embarrassment.

This is undoubtedly a possible side-effect of yoga
for some inexperienced yogis, and another potential
embarrassment is simply being too stiff to even *know*
you've got some of the places the teacher says you
have to wrap your legs round, let alone being able to
do it. But it shld not put off Teenage Worriers who
are attracted to Yoga, because it is a lifetime study
that can, in time, develop V. Good health and
suppleness of Bod, as well as a reduction ih the
symptoms of Worrying, which has to be A Good
Thing.

Some Yogis are supposed to have gained such
complete control over their bodies and minds that
they are not even susceptible to Banana, and live
very long lives. I'm not sure how much of a Good
Thing this is of course, because even though a vast
population of 900-year-old yogis might not eat very
much due to Self Discipline, or use much Fossil
Fuels Etck due to sitting in one place all the time

You've all heard of people chanting OM --but have you heard of HAM, YAM, RAM, VAM & LAM? No, these are not types of tinned nosh, but all YOGA werds. Find yr own CHAKRA and you'll never yearn for illegal drugges, so they say......

Don't try this at home - get a teacher.

going Ommmmmmmm (or possibly getting around by Thought Transference), they still have to have a little patch of earth to sit on somewhere, and if nobody suffered from Banana at all, it would eventually get used up and they'd all have to sit on each other's heads like those motorbike acts in the circus.

ZOMBIE

Zombie comes, according to the Dict. from a West African word 'zumbi', meaning 'fetish'. I don't think this means, however, that zombies are people who go around in rubber flippers, or like being chained up and coated with strawberry mousse Etck, but the orig. meaning of Fetish, which is something worshipped for magick powers. (Well, come to think of it, that's probably what the strawberry mousse people reckon too . . .) Zombies were Ded Bods, supposedly brought back to Life by Ancient Magick, so that's why we use the word to mean V. Slow-witted, dull or inert Person, hard to tell from Ded Bod except by V. Close medical examination.

There have been times when even the V. Nice and Generous-Hearted El Chubb has concluded that Adored Father is a Zombie, but usually when he has consumed aforementioned industrial-strength Trappist Monk lager and then thinks he is imparting V. Imp Deep Truth about The Universe,

ZOMBIES? Nope. Just perfectyl NORMAL Teenage Worriers like U & Me, who have stayed up all night working V.V.V. Hard for insane have-it-all society's vile exams. End this tyranny, sez L.Chubb.

which takes the form of a long, strange noise that goes 'fwwlerrrryyuurrnnnnn'.

Whether we use a Werd like Zombie or not, most of us, Teenage Worriers or otherwise, have been tempted to conclude there is absolutely nothing going on inside the Hed or Bod of somebody we know and prob don't like, but Ancient Rune about not judging a book by its cover is worth bearing in Minde. It is also possible that somebody we think is a Zombie and worthy only of ridicule Etck is akshully suffering from Depression (see DEPRESSION) and needs expert help. And another thing – if the Zombie really does turn out to be a Ded Bod brought back to Life by Ancient Magick Etck, it wld be better to stay on the right side of them because from what I hear from Ashley of videos like *Night of the Living Ded* Etck, they're often pretty cheesed off about being woken up.

Which, come to think of it, makes them even more like most Teenage WORRIERS

...And cats

84

AFTERWORD

And now dear readers, I bid you adieu, *having shared My Inner Worries, bared my Inner Soul, thrown myself on yr mercy Etck Etck, marred only by the sinking feeling (wish I'd never seen that Titanic movie) that I have but skimmed the V.V. tip of the iceberg and that all yr MIND and BODY Worries are still just as Deep and Unsolved and lurking underneath the ocean of yr swelling soul as they were when I began.*

Truth is, Worrying about our lives is part of what makes us human. I hate to admit it, but when I look at Rover, much as I adore her and worship ye ground on which her paws pad, I have to admit that her MIND and BODY and Worries seem confined to:

a) Food

b) Sleep

and even in this short list I'm not sure whether Worries are the right description, praps Needs is better . . .

But we humans are always moving the goalposts, seeing greener grass in distance Etck. We want something, we get it, then we want something else. I think there is good and bad in this. If we were all like Rover, I spose there'd be no wars, but also (sigh) no bukes, no paintings, no songs. Moi thinks, the Secret is to be a bit more like Rover, contented in the moment, and try to turn our Worrying bitz into creative bitz. This will prob take the rest of my life.

And we ask ourselves, does the purrfect harmony between MIND and BODY exist? My answer, dearest reader, is yes, briefly, for little moments. Now and then, everyone feels that their MIND and BODY are both completely relaxed, but they don't always notice. It often happens when you laugh . . . Treasure ye moments before ye grimme reaper of Glume cuts a swathe of festering pustules through yr bright horizon . . . And also, however deep the troughs of glume may be, remember that your little MIND and BODY will recover, and buoy you up on billowy waves of joy Etck. It's all part of life's rich tapestry.

Yrs truly, madly, deeply (heading for life of quiet contemplation or luney binne, depending on how well I can meditate). Sadly, my own MIND and BODY seem intent on sending large Worry waves through shuddering frame even as I write. Ommmmmmmmmmm. That's better . . . I feel a sneeze — or is it a Yawn? — coming on),

Letty Chubb x
x
x x

86

Help!

Useful telephone numbers for serious MIND & BODY Worries. There will probly be local numbers, too, in your phone directory. Remember that calls can show up on some itemized telephone bills. And don't forget yr doc shd have lots of helpful leaflets too that can help . . .

ALCOHOL/DRUGS

Drinkline
Helpline: 0345 320202
(Mon to Fri, 9.30 a.m. to 11 p.m.; Sat and Sun, 6–11 p.m., all calls charged at local rate)
Freephone 0500 801802 (recorded info)
Very helpful with advice on drinking levels Etck. Can send you a free book, 'The Big Blue Book of Booze'.

Department of Health
National Drugs Helpline
Freephone 0800 77 66 00
A free and confidential service open 24 hours a day, 365 days a year. Also available in a range of languages other than English. Free leaflets and literature.

EATING DISORDERS

Eating Disorders Association
01603 621414
Youth Helpline
(18 years and under):
01603 765050
(4-6pm only; recorded message at other times).
Publishes information, newsletters and has details of local services and support groups.

ACNE

Acne Support Group
0181 845 8776

SELF-HARM

42nd Street
4th Floor, Swan Buildings,
20 Swan St, Manchester, M4 5JW
0161 8320170

National Self-Harm Network
c/o Survivors Speak Out
34 Osnaburgh Street, London, NW1 3ND
0171 916 5472 or 0171 916 0825

MIND PROBLEMS

Young Minds
0171 336 8445
Parents Information Service: 0345 626376
*Works to promote the mental health of children and young people.
Can provide advice/leaflets on subjects such as Eating Disorders,
Depression, Bullying, Self-harm Etck.*

DISABLED

PHAB
0181 667 9443
Clubs for physically handicapped and able-bodied young people.

SPOD

0171 607 8851
Sex and disability helpline.

GENERAL HELP/
INFORMATION

The Samaritans
National Linkline: 0345 909090 (calls charged at local rate from
wherever you call).
*24-hour emergency service for the suicidal or despairing. A local number
will also be in your telephone book or can be obtained by calling the
operator. If in serious trouble, DO CALL.*

Youth Access
0116 2558763
*A service for all young people, referring them to independent local coun-
selling services/advice centres Etck.*